S
51
57

31924

№2

Southern Writing in the Sixties

POETRY

Southern Writing
in the Sixties

POETRY

Edited by
John William Corrington
Miller Williams

LOUISIANA STATE UNIVERSITY PRESS
BATON ROUGE

A. M. D. G.

Acknowledgments

THE EDITORS OF *Southern Writing in the Sixties* wish to thank the following magazines and book publishers (and, of course, the authors) for permission to reprint the designated poems. Rights in each case are reserved by the owner of the copyright:

American Scholar for "Victory," by Robert Watson, and "The Associate Professor Delivers an Exhortation to His Failing Students," by Miller Williams; *Audit* for "Kissing a Mechanical Ape," by Duane Locke; *Carleton Miscellany* for "Anonymous Drawing," by Donald Justice, and "Reflections on the Second Day of Spring," by Charles Wright; *Chrysalis* for "The Crap Game," by Alfred M. Lee; *Colorado Quarterly* for "The Dead of the Latest War," by Marion Montgomery; *Cyclotron* for "The Pendulum People," by Ruth Dawson; *Delta* for "Comment dit-on femme en anglais?" by Ruth Laney; *Delta Review* for "To My Cellmate, Helen," by John Freeman; *Epoch* for "Pavane in the Form of an Elegy," by Ronald Perry; *HIKA* for "I Am a Whore with a Glass Room," by Ruth Dawson; *Hollins Critic* for "For David Kendig, director of poverty" and "Presences," by Jane Gentry; *Intermission* for "The Backyard," by Duane Locke; *Mademoiselle* for "About Grampa, Who Died Poor," by Edsel Ford; *Motive* for "Comfort," by Ted-Larry Pebworth, and "Nat Turner in the Clearing," by Alvin Aubert; *New Campus Writing IV* for "The Consequences of Hannibal, Mo.," by Jeptha Evans, and "The Unloved," by Robert Canzoneri; *New Yorker* for "Reincarnation" and "Listening to Foxhounds," by James Dickey; *Oberlin Quarterly* for "Orpheus Opens His Morning Mail," by Donald Justice; *Poetry* for "Lines for a Crucifix" and "The Shellpicker," by Ronald Perry; *Prairie Schooner* for "To People Other Places, Gentlemen," by Charleen Whisnant; *Saturday Review* for "At the County Fair," by Edsel Ford, "The Druggist," by Larry Rubin, and "One Lion, Once," by Robert Canzoneri; *Shenandoah* for "December Love Song," by Henry Taylor; *Stolen Paper Review* for "Billboards Ceased Their Ballet," by Duane Locke; *Triptych* for "Entrance," by Paul Ramsey; *Wormwood Review* for "Kate," by William E. Taylor.

Alfred A. Knopf for "Glucose" and "Fall Practice," by Dabney Stuart from his *The Diving Bell* (1966); Southern Poetry Review Press for "The Circus Is Not Far Away," by Paul Ramsey from his *In an Ordinary Place* (1965); University of Nebraska Press for "The Dead of the Latest War" and "Now Is the Only Elegy for April," by Marion Montgomery from his *Dry Lightning* (1960), and for "The Druggist," by Larry Rubin from his *The World's Old Way* (1963); University of North Carolina Press for "Desert Fox" and "The Gargoyle," by R. H. W. Dillard from his *The Day I Stopped Dreaming About Barbara Steele and Other Poems* (1966); University of Texas Press for "Romantic," "Tiresias," and "Bathing Beauty," by George Garrett from his *The Sleeping Gypsy* (1958); Wesleyan University Press for "Gamecock" and "Reincarnation," by James Dickey from his *Buckdancer's Choice* (1965) and for "A Dog Sleeping on My Feet" and "Listening to Foxhounds," from his *Drowning With Others* (1962); for "The Tree of Silence," by Vassar Miller from her *Wage War on Silence* (1960); and for "Anonymous Drawing," by Donald Justice from his *Night Light* (1967).

Poems by three of the contributors appeared originally in volumes published by the Louisiana State University Press. They are: Henry Taylor's "A Blind Man Locking His House," from his *The Horse Show at Midnight* (1966); James Whitehead's "Delta Farmer in a Wet Summer," "One for the Road," and "For a Neighbor Child," from his *Domains* (1966); and Miller Williams' "The Associate Professor Delivers an Exhortation to His Failing Students," from his *A Circle of Stone* (1964).

Contents

x   *Contents*

Introduction

IN INTRODUCING *Southern Writing in the Sixties: Fiction*, we made reference to the similarities between the cultures of the South and New England. Not the least of these is the way in which fiction, which we are told followed far behind poetry in the first order of things, probably evolving out of it, was first in the order of things in both New England and the South. Hawthorne was writing when the only poetry around was an imitation of what had been done earlier in the mother country, and the prose of Melville was not equaled in poetry, nor often approached. Not for a long time would the mention of New England's writers bring to mind the poets: Edwin Arlington Robinson, Robert Frost, E. E. Cummings, or Elizabeth Bishop (except of course for Emily Dickinson, who is the exception in so many things that we become accustomed to including her out).

Just so in the South the field has belonged generally to the storytellers. Until the third decade of this century, the names of John Esten Cooke, Thomas Nelson Page, George Washington Cable, Joel Chandler Harris, and Ellen Glasgow, clearly no Melvilles, had no counterparts in poetry, unless we consider Edgar Allan Poe, and perhaps Sidney Lanier. The Southerner was getting a reputation as a good storyteller, but the poets were then in Concord or Boston or New York.

Then something happened. And what happened was John Crowe Ransom. And John Gould Fletcher. And Conrad Aiken. And Donald Davidson. And Allen Tate. And we can't forget

Maxwell Bodenheim. We looked one day and saw Fletcher from Little Rock, up there with the imagists, not imitating but experimenting, finally to become the best imagist of them all. About that time Mr. Aiken of Savannah published his first book. Max Bodenheim from Mississippi was on the road, down and out in Paris and London, when out of Nashville came suddenly the poems of Ransom, Davidson, Tate, Warren, and the fellow Fugitives. From that waking, that rushing around, the poetry from the South has come increasingly and considerably into its own.

Surely the continued work of these poets would have been sufficient to hold an important place for the poetry of the South in the nation's literature; and, excepting Ransom who turned primarily to criticism, each of them has kept on giving us poetry, and in good quantity. But these have been increased in number by two generations of younger poets from the South, until now, if the mention of Southern literature still brings to mind most generally William Faulkner—which certainly it ought to—with Eudora Welty, Carson McCullers, Flannery O'Connor, and William Styron, there are also James Agee, the poet, and Randall Jarrell, and in this volume, James Dickey, George Garrett, Donald Justice, Alfred M. Lee, Marion Montgomery, and others, all of them good poets.

But as significant as it is that there are this many, that they are good, writing hard and demanding to be read that way—as important as that is for the future of the South and its literature—it isn't necessary to read their biographies to know where they came from; the poems tell it. They tell it because the place is in them, and the sense of religion and the sense of history. Because they bring to form what we have talked about. It is the poetry of the South.

John William Corrington
Miller Williams

New Orleans
1966

Southern Writing in the Sixties

POETRY

ALVIN AUBERT

Bessie Smith's Funeral

The brief procession.
The crude gray church that pegs the bend
Of a river. After brisk December air

Smoke-white walls,
An artless trim of brown,
Windows unadorned
Except for what of fields beyond
The eye can trace on dusty panes.

Chafed by fiery oration
That rains on salamandered ears,
Naked bulbs retreat
From slaking so much darkness, turn
To dalliance with lilies and a casket
Textured to the dime-store toy that reins
The impish hands of a child close by.

Spirits are abroad in the splintery pews,
Restless in the drafty aisles, will not
Give way to order of service, to such
Superfluous mourning;

One, a burly chantress with a song,
Balks the yokeless choir that grates
The lily-scented air;
Her song is news, begins the dispensation
Of the blues.

Nat Turner in the Clearing

Ashes, Lord—
But warm still from the fire that cheered us,
Lighted us in this clearing where it seems
Scarcely an hour ago we feasted on
Burnt pig from our tormentor's unwilling
Bounty and charted the high purpose your
Word had launched us on. And now, my comrades
Dead, or taken; your servant, pressed by the
Blood-drenched yelps of hounds, forsaken, save for
The stillness of the word that persists quivering
And breath-moist on his tongue; and these faint coals
Soon to be rushed to dying glow by the
Indifferent winds of miscarriage—What now,
My Lord? A priestess once, they say, could write
On leaves, unlock the time-bound spell of deeds
Undone. I let fall upon these pale remains
Your breath-moist word, preempt the winds, and give
Them now their one last glow, that some dark child
In time to come might pass this way and, in
This clearing, read and know.

VAN K. BROCK

Spelunking

I killed the useless light
    And, fingers like snakes,
Crawled in hilly darkness.
        Earth's dark touched inside
Defied proportion. Shelves
        Dissolved. Stoning depths,
I splashed hidden rivers—
    Knowing of no hell,
That all circled nightmare,
    That panic crumbles
Earth. My leather whispers,
    Carousing like bats,
Echoed their own beings.
    Rules say sit and wait,
But this crazy cave kept
    Combing the cool earth.

In light's forgotten roots
    A headless hill bled
With a blue silver blaze
    And by its streams where
Orchards sprang from hidden
    Fruits, animals grazed.
While father searched earth, his
    Sun burning on his
Brow, there at last the sun
    And moon together
Shoaled my still-born sister,
    With a slight friend (struck
In youth by lightning) that
    Played with my dogs, names
Forgotten, including

The six-week puppy
My brother killed in wrath.
        We were all strangers,
Our lives over our heads.

Though the sounds of bats grew
        Slowly to cries and
I decided they were
        Not my own lost sounds,
I did not answer the
        Rescue crew at first.
My name in a stranger's
        Mouth was wrong, my voice
Echo to them whose hands
        Were colder than life;
And flesh in their lanterns—
        Even mine—was not
A known color. The roots
        Began to dissolve
In slow shock waves of day,
        And I felt myself
Swimming against the light
        (As in Plato's Cave)
Toward people who cheered when
        I emerged, although
They did not know what I
        Had found in earth; I
Was a stranger and they
        Looked for themselves or
Something they had buried.

The Encyclopaedia

When it arrived, I unpacked everything.
The room grew quiet. My years of higher learning
Seemed nothing. Here was knowledge ordered, a sectional
God—dried, packed, and shelved—the prank
Of computers. Inside those covers the pages, letters,
And ink wiggled, waiting, not a reading,
But a restoration to what was once a mind.
The fragments squirmed to give their secrets back.
I wanted to cry, "Murder!" because I thought
It possible. I searched the atlas for charts, the index
For keys to connections; I scanned the guides, exhausting
All directions, and finally the text, for hints.
I begot idiots and robots. Thrilled, I stalled,
Knowing I could destroy myself unless
I learned to release those facts through cooler reason.

Manacled by black fluid to white paper,
The invisible god, folded in imitation
Leather, attractively matches the furniture.
Insure against fire and wind, for when set free
He reverts to his former evil, ignorant nature,
Goes howling vacant darkness, whoring peasants
With faith, until they kneel at what they know,
Who never knew at all except with awe.

ROBERT CANZONERI

The Unloved

When I would squat by holes and piles of dirt
crumbling clods, ready to insert
bare roots of shrubs, she'd soil my vegetable dreams:
this adolescent dog approaching albino
would worm under my arm with motive I know
too but bury in pride, curl both head
and tail toward me begging to be fed
love at both extremes.

Neither was an end unto itself, or
small dogs one might do as well for;
a car front struck her fore part like a match
that spurts red fire and dies, curdled a batch
of blood out from one end and knocked
oval feces out the other. Shocked,
arrested at the waste, I swore a herbist
vow; but now I felt the still unserviced
bitch for lack of pulse and breath. I coiled
her limp into a hamper, saw it soiled
with drying blood. She stiffened in a curl,
never having learned a nicer girl
could hope to stay unspaded, yet behave.
With too much heat I dug a rounded grave.

One Lion, Once

Ho, Androcles!
What do you say went on
From when the lion scratched off in the dust
Toward you as meat and bone
And, roaring to his lean and hungry guts
The end of grumbling wait,
Bore down? What shifted in those preying eyes
As, closing, you grew featured
And the features made a face? What lies
Would not reach truth too late
But failed the heated lion's sight, as face
Became not one man's meat,
But Androcles?
We could ask Plato, looking back, to place
The abstract qualities
Of this into a scheme: how many rungs
Of love a beast can seize
In one great charge, to land (with rasping lungs
And flesh starved to his bones)
Muzzling like a milk-fed cat at ease
Against you on your knees.

RUTH DAWSON

I Am a Whore with a Glass Room

I am a whore with a glass room
At the bottom of a lake.
Neptune is impotent
And Proteus is broke
And all the rest
Are in love with mermaids.
Once in awhile when it rains
A poet drowns
And there are songs in my house
For a moment . . .
The sight of man to me is music
Though he be wet and dead,
He is the reason I was made—
I've never seen one
I didn't know: all cry.
We are bound by weakness.
Sometimes I am stronger
And catch and hold his face
Against the waterlilies
And admit that he is more beautiful
Than flowers; then again
He is the stronger
Just for being dead.
We stare at one another,
The sinking poet and I,
His hair streaming in the waters
And I, a whore, in a warm
Glass room at the bottom of nowhere.
We always ask one another why—?
I watch him die writhing for air
Among the shells.
And remember he is the reason

I was made
And then go to the other side of the room
And watch the starfish
Eat their children
Silently and without ceremony.

The Pendulum People

We walked the hills of Jerusalem
When the sun, high in the clouds
Caught the shadow of a cross.
We drank mead on the moors
Of Scotland when the moon
Shone on a stone prison.
We sang to lute music
When Caesar screamed his curses
In the marble halls of Rome.
And dancing for Creon
And rich Corinth merchants, we
Heard from a chorus of women
That Medea had slain her children.

Now they want us to call back
Things too old to remember.
Do they think that we, like they
Butcher time?
The clocks unwind an innocent thread
From loom to spool to dye;
Only the weaver's hands fumble going back,
And the judges multiply.
Christ and Mary and Caesar
And Medea's children, the last.
The sundials spoke then.
So let us pass.
Let us pass.

JAMES DICKEY

Gamecock

Fear, jealousy and murder are the same
When they put on their long reddish feathers,
Their shawl neck and moccasin head
In a tree bearing levels of women.
There is yet no thread

Of light, and his scabbed feet tighten,
Holding sleep as though it were lockjaw,
His feathers damp, his eyes crazed
And cracked like the eyes
Of a chicken head cut off or wrung-necked

While he waits for the sun's only cry
All night building up in his throat
To leap out and turn the day red,
To tumble his hens from the pine tree,
And then will go down, his hackles

Up, looking everywhere for the other
Cock who could not be there,
Head ruffed and sullenly stepping
As upon his best human-curved steel:
He is like any fierce

Old man in a terminal ward:
There is the same look of waiting
That the sun prepares itself for;
The enraged, surviving-
another-day blood,

And from him at dawn comes the same
Cry that the world cannot stop.

In all the great building's blue windows
The sun gains strength; on all floors, women
Awaken—wives, nurses, sisters and daughters—

And he lies back, his eyes filmed, unappeased,
As all of them, clucking, pillow-patting,
Come to help his best savagery blaze, doomed, dead-
game, demanding, unreasonably
Battling to the death for what is his.

A Dog Sleeping on my Feet

Being his resting place,
I do not even tense
The muscles of a leg
Or I would seem to be changing.
Instead, I turn the page
Of the notebook, carefully not

Remembering what I have written,
For now, with my feet beneath him
Dying like embers,
The poem is beginning to move
Up through my pine-prickling legs
Out of the night wood,

Taking hold of the pen by my fingers.
Before me the fox floats lightly,
On fire with his holy scent.
All, all are running.
Marvelous is the pursuit,
Like a dazzle of nails through the ankles,

Like a twisting shout through the trees
Sent after the flying fox

Through the holes of logs, over streams
Stock-still with the pressure of moonlight.
My killed legs,
My legs of a dead thing, follow,

Quick as pins, through the forest,
And all rushes on into dark
And ends on the brightness of paper.
When my hand, which speaks in a daze
The hypnotized language of beasts,
Shall falter, and fail

Back into the human tongue,
And the dog gets up and goes out
To wander the dawning yard,
I shall crawl to my human bed
And lie there smiling at sunrise,
With the scent of the fox

Burning my brain like an incense,
Floating out of the night wood,
Coming home to my wife and my sons
From the dream of an animal,
Assembling the self I must wake to,
Sleeping to grow back my legs.

Listening to Foxhounds

When in that gold
Of fires, quietly sitting
With the men whose brothers are hounds,

You hear the first tone
Of a dog on scent, you look from face
To face, to see whose will light up.

When that light comes
Inside the dark light of the fire,
You know which chosen man has heard

A thing like his own dead
Speak out in a marvelous, helpless voice
That he has been straining to hear.

Miles away in the dark,
His enchanted dog can sense
How his features glow like a savior's,

And begins to hunt
In a frenzy of desperate pride.
Among us, no one's eyes give off a light

For the red fox
Playing in and out of his scent,
Leaping stones, doubling back over water.

Who runs with the fox
Must sit here like his own image,
Giving nothing of himself

To the sensitive flames,
With no human joy rising up,
Coming out of his face to be seen.

And it is hard,
When the fox leaps into his burrow,
To keep that singing down,

To sit with the fire
Drawn into one's secret features,
And all eyes turning around

From the dark wood
Until they come, amazed, upon
A face that does not shine

Back from itself,
That holds its own light and takes more,
Like the face of the dead, sitting still,

Giving no sign,
Making no outcry, no matter
Who may be straining to hear.

Reincarnation

Still, passed through the spokes of an old wheel, on and around
The hub's furry rust in the weeds and shadows of the
                    riverbank,
This one is feeling his life as a man move slowly away.
Fallen from that estate, he has gone down on his knees
And beyond, disappearing into the egg buried under the sand

And wakened to the low world being born, consisting now
Of the wheel on its side not turning, but leaning to rot away
In the sun a few feet farther off than it is for any man.
The roots bulge quietly under the earth beneath him;
With his tongue he can hear them in their concerted effort

To raise something, anything, out of the dark of the ground.
He has come by gliding, by inserting the head between stems.
Everything follows that as naturally as the creation
Of the world, leaving behind arms and legs, leaving behind
The intervals between tracks, leaving one long wavering step

In sand and none in grass: he moves through, moving nothing,
And the grass stands as never entered. It is in the new
Life of resurrection that one can come in one's own time
To a place like a rotting wheel, the white paint flaking from it,
Rust slowly emerging, and coil halfway through it, stopped

By a just administration of light and dark over the diamonds
Of the body. Here, also naturally growing, is a flat leaf
To rest the new head upon. The stem bends but knows the
    weight
And does not touch the ground, holding the snub, patterned
    face
Swaying with the roots of things. Inside the jaws, saliva

Has turned ice cold, drawn from bird eggs and thunderstruck
    rodents,
Dusty pine needles, blunt stones, horse dung, leaf mold,
But mainly, now from waiting—all the time a symbol of evil—
Not for food, but for the first man to walk by the gentle
    river:
Minute by minute the head becomes more poisonous and
    poised.

Here in the wheel is the place to wait, with the eyes unclosable,
Unanswerable, the tongue occasionally listening, this time
No place in the body desiring to burn the tail away or to warn,
But only to pass on, handless, what yet may be transferred
In a sudden giving-withdrawing move, like a county judge
    striking a match.

R. H. W. DILLARD

Desert Fox

for C. W. Parker

The general knows. His maps
Spread on the table, creases
And all. And his pointer ceases
To make sense, just waggles up
And down. But he knows.

The grumble of the idling
Tanks below the window.
Their guns are muffled
Canvas in the dust.

"Must we always assault
From the rear, when most
Often a frontal thrust
Meets with the least
Opposition?" His heels
Click convulsively.
The colonels nod. His mind
Is clearly elsewhere.

Not there
But in the general's bed,
No Mata Hari, the English
Spy reclines. Miranda,
Pale and blue and yellow,
Her hair pressed to his
Pillow, her legs bare
Beneath the starched flat
Sheet, her breasts, arms,
Shoulders naked in the air,

His hollow room. Her teeth
Are small and round and sharp.

When will he move, arch a finger
On the map, alert the tanks
For a full advance? His eyes
Are closed, his pointer
Clatters to the floor. He sighs.

Her nervous tongue advances
The hollows of her lower
Lip, tips in and out.

A shout in the swirling sand,
The canvas rips as muzzles raise,
The general stalks the empty room,
His eyes lit, thoughts of the pass,
The plunging charge, the clash,
The grapple with the foe.

Bang, maps on the floor,
The double door snaps to,
A frightened aide,
The general in the sand
Who bellows in the wind,
Turns in the sand,
Stands in the turning sand.
He contemplates
A victory for the fatherland.

Her fingers tap his name
In Morse along her thigh,
Assault soon to begin,
Her job, his boots
Beyond the door.

A tank antenna whips
The wind.

Another win,
Another loss, toss
Of the sheets from head
To toe. He knows
The maps, lay of the land

As pale Miranda
Watches his advance
And nips her thumb.

The Gargoyle

The evening sun fell
Black against the sky
Soot streaked the wrinkled stones
And eyes glinted from the narrow panes.

The singing master's reply,
Low and monotonous,
The spire,
Still suspended atilt above the walls,
The pinpoint fires,
And the gypsy camp far in the hills.

"We have waited for four weeks
And the weather has not abated;
The master masons have retired
And St. Fina alone remains."

The echoes that rupture the stone silence,
The mown fields,
The naked trees
Brazen in the sunset,
While the screaming birds
Circle and wheel,
Afraid to light.

JEPTHA EVANS

The Consequences of Hannibal, Mo.

Hannibal, Mo. announces the opening
Of the Mark Twain Shopping Center. My sister Mary
Announces her divorce. I have a severe rectal pain
That could be cancer. Through the window
The moon collapses onto the living room floor.
Outside, on the lawn, drunk students laugh and shout.
It's like a nightmare or the neighbors
Watering their odoriferous lilacs.

I step onto the fire escape, scream to the students:
"Next time you're in Hannibal, don't forget to visit
The Mark Twain Shopping Center. I'm dying
Of cancer." Shouts, laughter. My sister Mary. "Yes," I said,
"It's for the best. We all die sooner or later." My father
Agreed. Some people have heart trouble in their heads.
But the moonlight, and these severe pains in the rectum,
For days now. Or weeks? "It's for the best," he said.

The odor of lilacs pervades the room
Like a nightmare. I step onto the fire escape.
Yesterday six men were shot on the streets of Nassau.
I'm afraid of what a doctor might say, but yesterday . . .
Outside, on the front lawn, a frenzied sorority girl
Screams something about the Mark Twain Shopping Center.
I wonder. Is this the end after all? Moonlight!
"My sister Mary," I begin loudly. Shouts, laughter.

JEAN FARLEY

Charity Performance

"The eleven year old Siamese twins from San
Francisco, who have dedicated their talents to God,
will sing tonight at the Second Baptist Church."
—HATTIESBURG (MISS.) AMERICAN

Into a silence as stiff as greed
Intrude two wary heads.
Avoiding the puckered faces
Which burst into flower before them,
They watch the hidden spaces
For something as reticent, say,
As a small green head—
A weaving, doubling deed in their path
Signing, I am the snake and the grass;
This steady golden eye,
No more knowing than known,
Is the crystal of perfect flesh
Which all of us bear.
Watch courteously there until, outside
Or inside, creatures may sing in their grass;
You in your sunshine
And I in my shade
Will be the two sides of Siamese twins,
Eleven years old from San Francisco—
To whom nothing in the world is strange.

EDSEL FORD

At the County Fair

Armed with some merciless notions, the high school band
Ambushed Sousa outside the poultry building,
Seeing, as it were, the whites of the eyes
Of twenty village queens in pastel formals,
Each with her pastel heart set on the crown:
Miss Benton County Fair of 1960.

In the pigeon cages, a general rout ensued.
The pouters pouted, the fantails fanned, the
Trumpeters trumpeted loud and long.
The nuns and helmets claimed immunity
By their vestures, and what's more:
The archangels wondered who in hell
Had stolen their thunder and jumped Judgment Day.
The English carriers carried on, if not in English;
The racing homers would have raced home gladly
Except for U.S. Steel which does a prison make.
The tumblers tumbled. A magpie croaked Retreat.

Shall I report that the new queen fell on her face?
That the M.C. was exiled for certain unmanly remarks?
That a child of six picked the locks on the pigeon cages—
Or the band, forty strong in brand-new uniforms,
Fell into a chasm which opened miraculously?

No; but a moment later the CofC
Manager was seen to snap an old lady's head off,
And, wondrous to tell, her body was borne up
By two white sacred doves who through it all
Had kept their peace, though they had won
Nothing at all, not even a white ribbon.

About Grampa, Who Died Poor

My grandfather in his once-Spenserian hand
cribbed by the cold which scotched his ancient bones
wrote two-cent postcards out of Dixieland
to twenty kin and near-kin, Smith and Jones
and several mixed up of a foreign name,
saying *Now I am free, I might arrange a trip* . . .
ready to travel before the postman came:
clothes in a parcel, medicines in a grip.
But those who answered said they had the flu
or were about to move or *Maybe later;*
and he having nothing nothing whatever to do
got too old even for the elevator,
much less the train . . . lamenting most, no doubt,
the forty cents it took to feel them out.

JOHN FREEMAN

To My Cellmate, Helen

"Will no other vice content you?"
JOHN DONNE, *The Indifferent*

We have it that our vice of bodies began
With light fingered gentry on the skins
Who pinch the apple, spiked in the broad limbs.
Disease embodied in the mad fruit rants:

"Man will be Adam whose bone rose in the waters,
His judgment steeped in juices festered by sin;
He reels to the swamp in the valley of his fathers
Where flesh is angry for its origin."

Then came the warden with the biting Word,
Whose sentence fit too tight the walls on my jail;
And you, my friend of feelings, he drove with his sword
From flowers to the cramp of sides in your cell.
We are love's inmates locked in an angry vise
Who suffer knowledge in the crowding thighs.

GEORGE GARRETT

Romantic

I've heard some jealous women say
that if your skin were cut away
and tacked upon a public wall
it would not please the eyes at all.

They say your bones are no great prize,
that hanging in the neutral breeze
your rig of ribs, your trim of thighs
would catch no fetching harmonies

but tinkle like a running mouse
over piano keys. They hold
that, stripped, your shabby soul
will whimper like a vacant house

you are so haunted. "Ask
her," they say, "if she'll unmask.
Let her shed beauty like winter trees.
Time will bring her to her knees."

Still, I must have you as you are,
all of a piece, beautiful and vain,
burning and freezing, near and far,
and all my joy and all my pain.

And if you live to scrub a floor
with prayer, to weep like a small ghost,
which of us will suffer more,
who will be wounded most?

Tiresias

Speak to us who
are also split.
Speak to the two
we love and hate.

You have been both
and you have known
the double truth
as, chaste, obscene,

you were the lover
and the loved.
You were the giver
who received.

Now tell us how
we can be one
another too.
Speak to us who

in single wrath
cannot be true
to life or death.
Blinder than you.

Bathing Beauty

The sun, this morning
scored for trumpets, blares
over the sculptured gestures of
bathers in bright costumes.

They are untouched.
Only gulls and children fly
for pure joy to the holy noise.
Older we warm by the tune

like the blind by a roaring
fire. Cat-sleek, curled
in knowledge of herself,
dozing in the dazzle,

she has caught my eye.
I see her on a scallop shell
or lounging in the perfect lines
of a Matisse.

O Suzanna, I'll
stand on tiptoes, breathless
among the frozen elders. O
Judith, here's my head

my heart my four limbs
and my balls and all
(O Ruth) my alien corn.
She stretches, sighs, and seems

to be asleep. I shut my eyes
to hear the gulls and children
sing. I hear my voice
wailing by an ancient wall.

The sun, all trumpets, blares
and the sea is falling, falling
like the walls of Jericho
whose waves are tongues of dust.

JANE GENTRY

For David Kendig, director of poverty

I was
barely five years old
when my aunt magic gave me
a golden purse
slung on a golden chain
and hung with golden beads.

Beneath her flame-green trees,
jostled by the throngs of grass
I spent its gold
on bargain days in sheds and barns,
inside the oak, beneath the porch,

and, finally, in the outhouse:
the purse, flickering, fell.
Forever dropped, it lay
on the bottom
of the straight dark pit,
far to reach, near to see:
dead eye glinting in the excrement.

Since
(years fallen through fingers),
I've spent my purse
(golden and regained in dreams)
time and again;
given my gold into the laps
of one, two, many
who don't count, who keep the change

who leave me stranded, tiptoeing,
beside a high-lashed eye

staring at the golden purse
studded, glowing, in the mire.
Interested in first cause and curse,
I worship: fallen tongue on fire.

Presences

I thought my father callous, my mother hard,
And my grandfather unfeeling above all
For not being wretched when an old road moved
Or when a house or barn would burn or fall.

That far child loved old things,
Worshipped past because she had none.
But to change from child, she learned
As those who got her learned:
When sight goes empty through the vacant air—
The landmark gone—
Its absence is more ancient than its being there.

EDWIN GODSEY

One for the Road

I laid no siege and brought no 3-ton ram
To starve you out or batter in the door.
You didn't need the cannon where I came.
You knew, honey, I was no chevalier.

So our Great Troy was won with espionage.
I paid for the drinks, whispered, found my traitress,
And so with her assistance wired the bridge.
The mayor wept, reading his press release.

But every burg has got its ruins—its gout
In suburbia, pleuritic factories,
Malignant slums, thrombosis in Main Street.
The slabs go down on crowded cemeteries.

Woman, there were nine strata of Ilioses.
Helen's was burned. The others fell to pieces.

JEAN JEFFRIES

Circus

I think I've seen that trick before,
grin-weary clowns strewing paper water,
the acrobat displaying vague scars of tedium,
that same moss-eared juggler
wondering if the check will cover the car,
tossing hoops of red and green
into the gray air.
Faces gulp the fliers swinging slow
parabolas. Only in a darkened aisle
do the balloon man's meteorite eyes
breed sparks of chaos.

In His Room

Among exact connotations of ether and white
and the tinfoil cross on the wall,
this future survivor searches memory, looking for
something. And finds there your sins.

Grandfather, I will forget this room,
the face of the nurse who comes just now
to feed the tissued flowers whose roots
are already dead, that fine mist of hope
the doctors bring to lull us back to death,
and your poor old fingers
fumbling for one more day.

But when even your emptied rooms have healed
how do I forget
the sudden guilty look we traded?

DONALD JUSTICE

Anonymous Drawing

A delicate young Negro stands
With the reins of a horse clutched loosely in his hands;
So delicate, indeed, that we wonder if he can hold the spirited
    creature beside him
Until the master shall arrive to ride him.
Already the animal's nostrils widen with rage or fear.
But if we imagine him snorting, about to rear,
This boy, who should know about such things better than we,
Only stands smiling, passive and ornamental, in a fantastic
    livery
Of ruffles and puffed breeches,
Watching the artist, apparently, as he sketches.
Meanwhile the petty lord who must have paid
For the artist's trip up from Perugia, for the horse, for the boy,
    for everything here, in fact, has been delayed,
Kept too long by his steward, perhaps, discussing
Some business concerning the estate, or fussing
Over the details of his impeccable toilet
With a manservant whose opinion is that any alteration at all
    would spoil it.
However fast he should come hurrying now
Over this vast greensward, mopping his brow
Clear of the sweat of the fine Renaissance morning, it would
    be too late:
The artist will have had his revenge for being made to wait,
A revenge not only necessary but right and clever—
Simply to leave him out of the scene forever.

Orpheus Opens His Morning Mail

Bills. Bills. From the mapmakers of hell, the
repairers of fractured lutes, the bribed judges
of musical contests, etc.

A note addressed to my wife, marked: *Please Forward*.

A group photograph, signed: *Your Admirers*. In their
faces a certain sameness, as if "ɪ" might, after
all, be raised to some modest power. Likewise in
their costumes, at once identical and transparent,
like those of young ladies at some debauched semi-
nary. Already—such is my vice—I have invented
the rooms in which they must once have locked themselves to read, as they say, my works: those barren
cells, beds ostentatiously unmade . . . the pinched
chrysanthemums, memorializing in a corner some
withered event . . . the mullioned panes, high up,
through which they have spied, far off, the shorn
hedge behind which a pimply tomorrow crouches, ex-
posing himself. O lassitudes!

Lastly, an invitation to attend certain rites to be
celebrated, come equinox, on the riverbank. I am
given to understand that I shall be guest of honor.
As always, I conceive the scene in advance: the
dark . . . the guards, tipsy as usual, sonorously snoring . . .
the fitful illumination of ankles, whitely flashing . . .
a rustling, suddenly, among the reeds . . . and then—then
I shall probably be asked to recite my *poems*. But
O my visions, O vertigoes! Do I imagine it only,
the perverse gentility of their shrieks?

RUTH LANEY

Comment dit-on femme en anglais?

If I were to come down a polished corridor
Wearing a white dress
With all of Phaedra
And Eve
And the woman-who-heals
Behind me
With all of history
Of wine and bread and wilderness
Of smiles and scents and words
Would there be flowers for me at the end?
Would there be a white room
a red velvet bed?
Would I smell cut grass from the arching windows?
Would silk rustle or violins sing?
    Or would there be only
    what woman must receive and
    knows she must receive only?
A cave and a fire and a man
Who built the fire and carved the
Cave, and gives her not flowers,
Not velvet, not silk or violins, but
Only his hands and a fire in a cave?

ALFRED M. LEE

Maremma mi fe; disfecemi Maremma

Yap your outlandish language, lady; speak
your mind at the long paws and foreign talk
I jive you with, but breathe against my cheek.
A history of blue-eyed phrases smothers
this gagged battalion with a cloud of chalk.
I am more a man than your perfumed brothers.

Unwoplike pale, you make me think of pale
combatants that I shot at and the swarms
I should've slashed the skins off of. O jail
me—try me—kill me—kiss me there O there!
Over this slough, over these uniforms
no flag is coloring the malarial air.

Your perfumed brothers turn their manicured
and grinning palms both ways as if they'd won
with good manners the future I've endured
for far too long. But debts are overdue
in markets blacker than their moneyed one:
America takes Livorno; I make you.

No flag will show them where to when they come
to hang Nat Turner; they'll hang him anyway.
I've greased my rifle like you've greased my gun.
I testify by these that I am free
to make men die and die in disarray.
Feel it deep, sugar; die like a dog like me.

The Crap Game

Riding high on the lumbering elephants
    of their signed names, here come the young men
        lean with fawn-colored hair and
    blue eyes, who never think of money
but glide manfully among the high branches,

where fruit hangs. This sunlit April from flame trees
    they pick flowers, and elsewhere mangoes
        for their sisters and girlfriends,
    those lovely women who become so
from good food, soft beds, the very best dentists,

and the willingness of beautiful women
    to marry others than my father.
        My name and I are Frank Roach,
    and I drive a used car through this town
where so many line the roadside looking off

at the white-topped mountains moving through the palms.
    Behind a beerjoint my friends kneel down
        shooting craps so that a ghost
    might intervene and gather the bills
to one of them only, that he might purchase

a used elephant. Oh, we have bills enough.
    Where we watch the certainty of odds
        rattling among intentions,
    it is five-fifteen and after work
except for that one, who each morning shaves, makes

a funny sound with his tongue, and walks around
    all day, to the park, the river, here.
        His wife is with her mother.
    What was five minutes ago the noise
of a street crowd is the voice on the jukebox

on the other side of the door. Not a honk
or hooray disrupts our afternoon.
Shadows are long, straight, and cool
while I imagine the ice cold beers
of one more summer. It's not a bad life, just

Frank Roach's, who is still a young man. My son,
if he is born, never will shoot craps
far away in Nevada
with croupiers, but in this alley
where he'll miss his point. This is no gainful game

for an honest man. To roll is to keep faith
in yourself beyond what you bring here,
but you take away nothing.
At the near end of the alley
a procession of shadows hurries the twilight.

DUANE LOCKE

Kissing a Mechanical Ape

On the side street near the discount house, I saw
a man of marriageable age kissing a mechanical ape.
Then this same man began hugging himself.
I asked, "What does this mean?"
He replied, "I refuse to destroy my emblem by reasoned
        discourse,"
and he continued to hug himself.
This is a strange neighborhood, I thought,
I am returning to main street where there are traditional stores.
When I arrived each store was having a founder's day sale,
and I saw a thousand men in silkish suits,
each man hugging himself, and in silkish dresses
a thousand women each hugging her children.

Billboards Ceased Their Ballet

Billboards ceased their ballet,
and on the stage came a senile magician with no memory
of what he had promised us in our prehensile youth.
He reached into a betrayed rabbit, but no
mermaids handcuffed to diamonds descended
down steps woven from money dictaphones,
no footpaths of coins, confetti of smiles, or closets of illicit
        pajamas.

Only the screams of the rabbit were heard.
When he waved his wand again,

a city of cans appeared
where minutes with eye patches hurried down
the damp street of death that has no red light.

The Backyard

The backyard is filled
with lemon trees
and a temporary blue-gray small bird.

In the shadows
a steering wheel
is telling the children
long stories
of how to arise
out of a police sea
of shaving cream.

Their ears are
swimming in the automobiles
of tomorrow's padded air.

VASSAR MILLER

The Tree of Silence

Upon the branches of our silence hang our words,
Half-ripened fruit.
Gone are the months of summer, gone
Beyond pursuit.
Let us leave, though pinched and wan,
The windfalls wither
Under the tree whose shade affords
No shelter either.

For when was language ever food for human yearning!
Sun-gilded rain
Mocking the sheen of golden peach,
Words only drain
Hearts of strength; let mortal speech
Make time and way
For life, the long and lonely learning
How to pray.

De Profundis

O Lord, defend me when I go
through the dark in daylight.
Be with me when I smile peaceably
though tigers tear at my guts.

Stay with me who talk to my friends
as an earless monster

winks at me; comfort me, starved and black-tongued,
though I eat at dainty tables.

Stand by when snowfalls of words melt in
deserts of my deafness.
Sustain me, though morning after morning,
I take life from you like death.

Accept me, though I give myself
like a cast-off garment
to a tramp, or like an idiot's
bouquet of onions and roses.

MARION MONTGOMERY

The Dead of the Latest War

Hear our brief obsequies, repent for us
Who lived uneasy with the ash-dry taste
Of death upon our lips and came to waste
Before we came to seed; stark and wondrous
Old battles were denied, the ominous
And hateful enemy we never faced;
He was to us, and we to him, lines traced
On an electric screen. Now pity us.
There came no Priam seeking his slain son
When we were slain; Achilles was no more,
Or if he was, turned to a deadly thumb
That struck ten curved miles off, and if he won
His Troy he never saw its walls; this war
Struck Atreus' sons and Priam forever dumb.

Now Is the Only Elegy for April

The sag of forty years on pink bones, or the comfort of a
    withered foot toward Eden, is not equal to the sadness
    of the last joy of a season:

Only the last shrill December puff the voice makes, trailing
    frightened rabbits on white hillsides,
Only the last quick breath that enfolds once only the
    brown morning of October,
Only the tingling of that last deep green desire turned out
    of August backward to the multified greens

Can sing an elegy fullblooded as a girl with quick brown
  arms, shrill teeth,
And hair oily as the green moss in the river.

HARRY MORRIS

They Haint Nothin' Stupider'n a Cow Less'n Hit's a Chicken

I once had a cow named Isabella who fell
In love with my tractor. She came under the spill
Of the moon one night it was full, and those sixty-inch wheels
Raised a broad and potent hump and planted heels

Firm for the push. I couldn't plow but what
She'd follow; and, unlike any other stock,
A turn that brought me down a furrow right
Road for her budged her not a bushel bait.

I almost plowed her good those times and whiles
She showed her thing to me and twitched her tail.
I found her dead one night I couldn't sleep
(The moon full), near the tractor all aheap.

TED-LARRY PEBWORTH

Comfort

Those who own
You have lost

Touch trying to tell
Us how to think and

Feel joyless in our
Lust and even guilty in our

Love causing us to ignore
You or put to better use the

Word propping open
Windows in cheap

Hot hotels with
Gideons.

The Third Day

They resurrected
You a convenient
Hour after sun
Rise in the college
Stadium led by three
Ministers of major
Wasp persuasions with

Assistance from a high
School chorus and a
Lent electric organ in
The standard message
He is risen carried to
The shut ins on a rock
And roll establishment
Sponsored by city wide
Civic clubs combined
Catholics and several
Jews and all

This yet I am
Still in the same arena
Stalked by old lion
Hunger.

RONALD PERRY

Lines for a Crucifix

All day, in the gilded suit of skin he built,
My Christ hangs on the wall and sings
His sad songs, whereon the ornamental roses wilt,
And spill their bloody petals down.
Dazzled by promise, taken by surprise,
Two iron-witted, thieving kings
Prop him up, only to pull him down
At dark, and bury him under their eyes.

You've heard how he surprised the crafty Wise
Men, matching to their wits his child?
Learn now the matchless woodcraft of his eyes,
Their dusty ambiguities.
See how his bones, all Wise Men's ruin,
Under the cracked and skin-tight gold of his leaves
Are changing now, from the bones of the child
To the cross-shaped man, all Mankind's ruin.

This is the promise for which he grieves
And goes, in a wind, in a world so full of turning
There is no returning, but only the burning
Eyes of these two iron-fisted kings.
Shall they attest to his humanity
By dying, and thereby claim their own?
The roses rain their petals down
And make his blood, no longer his, their own.

But how shall these kings atone? He sings?
They cannot hear him. He downs? They prop
Him up, and drink his eyes, and cannot stop
Until his rose of thorns unlocks, and spills
Its obscure, scarlet sermons down.

See how they tangle for his crown.
Each king, for love, the other kills.
Each spills the other's blood upon the ground.

And thus fulfilled, of which he told
Who's speechless now, weighted gold
And with a heavy tongue that's not his own:
As still the roses rain their petals down
He hangs upon the wall and sings
His late and lonely madrigals,
To your, and all the world's surprise,
Who bury him perpetually in your eyes.

The Shellpicker

This lady, curled like a shell
In her work of love, picks
And pokes at everything. All
The long tide's wilderness
Is grief she touches to tell
How the blazing fish fall
Impossibly down, and the press
Of fathoms under the shell
Pours color up, or locks
The world in a diving bell
As water-shaped and delicate
And full of sound as a shell.
She knows the mysterious, deep
Music that the creatures tell
In rainbows, but in her sleep
The salt sea-weed is all
She catches in her net
Of hands. The fire-fish fall
Up to drown, as tenuous
And insubstantial as the coral

Strikes its flower, or the sun
Prints the smallest shell
With fire, or furious, hacks
Out long lightnings to tell
Its weaving watery shape
Up the Atlantic waves. Small
As any creature in her sleep,
Her hands feed on the shell.
For love she is undone,
And deep as the drowned bell
At death dives to a miracle,
The long sun in her sleep
Becomes a wilderness to tell
The perfect secret of her shape,
This lady, curled like a shell.

Pavane in the Form of an Elegy

How can I make an elegy
For her when she is not dead
Until tomorrow in the nursery-
Rhyme she cowered and read
As a child in a blue window?
Is it enough to speak for the dead
Who walk through the low
Gardens on crutches, weaving
In her crooked dreams like snow
Falling, like leaves, grieving,
Beside themselves at the death
She made them do, believing
The world was nothing less
Than a vision in her cramp?
How can I write her death
Into the wind when the hump-

Backed cripple knows his fix,
And tramples her under his stump?

Her eyes are clawed by a fox-
Eyed prince; her heart
Is ripped by a gardener's picks;
The roses twist and start
At her step; a witch's oven
Blooms at her heart.

Because as a child she was driven
To dark in a twitching fright,
She locks herself now in a prison
Of birds, and shutters the light
With an intricate window
That slices the terrible night
Into stars, insects, snow-
Creatures whirling under
The street. But she will grow
Down to a knowledge of wonder,
Deeper than she is buried,
When the moon rides under
The street. She will be married
To her fox-eyed prince,
As soon as she is buried,
In the ghost of a dance.

Her eyes will find the shape
Of a leaf; her hands
Will tug at the roots that snap;
Under the house, the surgery
Of stems will cut her shape.

PATRICIA RACHAL

Four Poems

A car hit mine
from the back
I never told
how that impact
released my neck
three-hundred
and sixty
free degrees.
I spin it
only at night
alone.
People frighten
easily.

Who designates
this blue beetle
beautiful?
(Maybe he waddles)

Who pronounces
that red, ugly?
(Maybe she pirouettes)

I prefer to race them
hooked like small oxen
butterflies.

Sir: Not up to
being minused for
incoherence
I cheated on your test.
I pretended to be
a face looking
over my shoulder.

Ice in a glass
is melting
It's cold outside
no crickets
Last summer they
were louder than
ever
I stayed awake
sounding them
The ice says:

Last year there was
a storm up north
We were snow
on a man
stranded
he fell
asleep.

PAUL RAMSEY

Entrance

What was, could.
If a bird's song rang
In a dark wood
And it took long
And the woods came
Leafy of game
Quick in a fear—
If a cry made
Its wet sound,
I stood there
In a frail air
Where a wind hid.
Then a stone sang.
Then the wind did.

The Circus Is Not Far Away

The circus soon. The mind drags
Childward, put upon, and slow.
It goes, does not want to go,
And yet arrives where time lags
In the bright disastrous air
Of an old and a known place
Mind would prefer not to face.
Do black horses tread that glare?
The manes flash and they are there.

LARRY RUBIN

The Druggist

He came to me last night, as if there had never
Been a box. Routine, no tales of Hell
To tell, he worked on an old prescription, and I
Watched, as I used to when I was a boy, and stifled
My eyes, and from the corner of his eye
He saw me and asked why. But all that dirt,
I said, how did you get up
Past all that dirt? I
Can pull pegs out with my teeth,
He said, and went on working.
Later, just before the third cock,
He handed me the jar. Son, he said,
I want you to deliver this before
You go. Is that all, I said, mustn't I
Avenge your death so you can rest? Just
Deliver that medicine, he said, and it was dawn
And of course he was gone. And I knew
That being sealed up like that had turned his wits,
Because I saw he had made the label out
To me.

JOSEPH EDGAR SIMMONS

Song of the Moth

It is your sweet propinquity
Spins my spirit's pinions to you.
Lovely flame, you I prefer
To the black dog scampering now at dusk
In corn and stubble—
These surely are flesh, and dog, he is the devil.
At least in your singeing I will sing
Fiery hozannahs better than mouthing clay.

Unpuzzle me my riddle of the mind:
Once I have reached you
I must reach you again—
O life-death
Your haughty couplings
Are brass distractions
At the open grave.

It is your warmth and light
—Silver arabesque of trope and strophe—
Tells me I need not lie down.
O death,
In your white throb
Tell me
Longing was not Faust's ruin.
Tell me
In your sacral scathing
The holy ghost is pinched to life.

Blonde Majorette:
Close-Up of Her Face on TV

Frown now
up at sun
take from sky
your flying baton.

The squirrely
freckles
on your face
are small suns whose
meaning baffles me
for I understand only
your love frown to sun

—this wheeling
freely slaving you—.

In your total commitment
to that matter in the sky
you cannot be ever masking, masking:
Voilà! Exposé complêt.
O pretty kitten
you are bitten
like sugar fed to eyes
rich plums in the glandstream.

Your vulnerable concert
like snake charmer
    lion tamer
    sun shooter
    beauty tragedienne
just misses
vulgarity.

Your act of concentration
(later fit for passion)
shows—

For this honesty I thank
your fear of public embarrassment
should you miss
your
my
the world's
baton.

MARCUS SMITH

Terminal Ward

And who could have predicted it?
Now,
This day of all my days;
Here,
Of all my places this place,
This remarkably dull room,
Its patient antiseptic air?

As if I never saw before
Something peels away.
The jaded eyes are innocent again
to the violating light.
I am a child.
There is chalky blue paint
And chalky pink paint,
The ceiling is a hieroglyph:
A mallard on a smudgy pond,
A leaf torn from its stem,
Always clouds and turtles,
Some familiar edge of face.

The others regard me quietly,
This bishop in his bed,
This duke of bottles and tubes.
The nurse bows low over my wrist
searching like a sorceress for a sign.
As in a church no one speaks:
They wait on me.

The uses of things belie their true integrity.
This blanket heavy on my knees like sod
This pillow a stone beneath my head

These clean starched pajamas:
When, where have they swaddled me before?

So should I say it's "like meeting an old friend"?
Or "I see Him sliding across the room
to take me by the hand"?
I think not.

Still with you, I begin to tell you less.
Allow me to be direct.

I shall be docile, accommodating, prompt.
The trivial unenduring instant
Will not pause for declamation.
It is coming, will be here,
Will pass.

Let us be charitable.
We only abolish each other a little bit
To know each other more.

DABNEY STUART

Fall Practice

Some after a night of sex, some hungover,
Some tanned, some fat, all still half asleep,
They'd sit around and give each other lip
Before padding up and cleating the summer clover
The field had grown to cover last season's dust.

"Her? Aw, man, that chick's a highway, I oughtta know,
I've driven it." "You gotta taste
That stuff, grow whiskers on your ass." "The best
I ever had was . . ." and so forth. The old show.
A bunch of scrubs bucking for first team berth.

I couldn't believe their talk. They'd cat all night
Yet next day hit the dummies, digging the turf,
Sweating, driving themselves for all they were worth
Into each other like bulls, brute against brute.
Whatever they got, girls, drunk, it wasn't enough.

It went on like that, late August through November.
Though I was the quarterback, the thinker
Who directed that beef, split ends, and set the flanker,
I worked at the center's butt, and I remember
Being primed for the big game, hungering for the cup.

Glucose

When I veined that quick syrup
The bottle hung above me
Like a sun. And now my father,
Tubed and pumped, in traction,
What sun does he see?

I call to him
Stranded six stories over
My head, *Father,*
Stranger, I wish I were hanging
Above you like a sun.

As it is, these white walls
Stare through me, an empty bottle
The nurses take pains
Not to break.

HENRY TAYLOR

December Love Song

Outside the diner, snow
    Muffles the lighted street.
You sit before me now,
And I, through smoke and steam,
    Stare at your lips, repeat
Not yours, but words I dream
    You send above the chink
    Of forks and plates. I shrink,

Become a boy of eight
    Perched on a washing machine:
Close to our inadequate
And antiquated radio,
    I dream my ears as keen
As those of stern-lipped Tonto
    Warning the Lone Ranger
    Of imperceptible danger.

All my childish wishes
    Concentrate on static,
The clatter of the dishes
In the sink before my mother,
    The roar of the automatic
Washing machine, all other
    Disruptive sounds that can
    Drown out the tall Masked Man

And the Indian, the sounds
    From Good and Bad Guys' guns.
My heart is out of bounds
Now, beyond the swinging door,
    Beyond cinnamon buns

Damp on the plate before
    Your eyes that try to reach
    Me, beyond attempts at speech,

Back with the drum of hooves,
    The note of recognition—
As the White Horse Silver moves
Across the plain, following
    The wind and the donation
Of the Bullet—in the bellowing
    Of one proud man who knows
    The Masked Man and tells those

Who wondered who this was
    Whose ringing voice is dying
Now. Outside, the snow is
Falling on the street, on eyes,
    The White Horse Silver, lying
On lips, your voice that tries
    To reach across this table, where
    It dies, drowned out in static air.

A Blind Man Locking His House

The tall clock in the hallway strikes
The half-hour chime:
Twelve-thirty. Now the hour has come
For footsteps in the dark, that like
To wander through this house from room to room.

My wife and I live here alone,
So my wife thinks;
But in the dark my dark eye blinks,
Down passageways of pure unknown
The hunter starts to stalk, and my heart sinks.

I rise and gird myself to face
This sounding house,
One hand stretched out against the blows
From chairs that will not stay in place,
From anarchy that sightlessness allows,

The other rummaging for keys
In my coat pocket.
At each door, as I pause to lock it,
Relentless blood assails my eyes
And drives them crazy: useless in their sockets,

They still roll upward in my head.
By force of will
I aim them downward: through this chill,
Pretending to look straight ahead,
I make the footsteps think I see, until

Between me and this heavy tread
At least one door
Is safely locked. From door to door
I pass, and learn I am misled:
There is no safe place for me any more.

To such thoughts does this presence tempt me
As floorboards creak
That I might drive myself to break
My heart at last, and find it empty,
Because some thing stalks me and will not speak.

The hallway clock clangs like my heart,
In time with feet
That flee, and press behind, and meet
At last, and all of this is part
Of all this house. My pitiful conceit

Breaks down, and I shall not escape.
Older than air
Or the stairway, he is somewhere
In dust and stone that saps all hope;
When I lie down that sound will still be there.

Time and again my wife has said
No one is there;
But in the weather of despair
As I climb up through dark to bed
I hear his step behind me on the stair.

WILLIAM E. TAYLOR

Kate

She refused, when the cancer came,
to dignify it with its name
and had pernicious anemia instead,
succumbing, occasionally, to bed.
Then, pinning the gaps up in her skirt,
she took her walks and hid the hurt
in her eyes when we would take our swim
or dig for clams. Even the prim
neatness remained and the English pride,
until the devil struck, and she died,
leaving to her nervous spouse
late liberty, and a quiet house.

ROBERT WATSON

Victory

Moving furniture around my room
I can move stars, the streetlights and the dust
In rolls below our chairs. I can change weather
If I want.

Changing the order of books in shelves
Christ marries Helen, Alexander leans
On Mother Goose. I can change all history
If I wish.

Putting on clothes I have not worn before
I sit on a shifted chair turning my body
To something new. I can be President
When I choose.

Opening the door to watch the snow
I walk frozen ground, past frozen trees,
Around the block, around. I can circle the universe
When I will.

Indoors I light a fire to warm the air,
I can move the chimney across the room,
Or doom the furniture in the hearth
If I please.

But you, like a frozen tree in frozen ground,
I'll walk around, I'll walk around the block,
I'll shift all the furniture in my room.
I'll move you yet.

The Judge Winds His Clock

"The Judge is dead.
The Judge is dead.
Throw him out the window
And spit on his head."

Each week I deal out years of jail.
Each year discard a life or two.
Each day for lunch a salad bowl.
(He sliced her head off in a fit;
She'd hid his shoes to keep him home)
Two bourbons evenings, never more.
I bathe at nine, I bed at ten,
I play croquet, cards, fish for trout.
(Law allows twelve fish in season)
The crimes men do. I see them all.
By now a million years of jail.
Inside a house, a cell of chairs,
We plotted crime 'til father set
Clock, wound sun, stars: his sentence bed.
Over our house, our cell, our crime,
The Grandfather's clock turns his face
To us, chimes his sentence for lunch,
Bourbon, bed, childhood, discarded lives.

All rise, eyes on me in black robes.
I strike my gavel, over-rule,
Spin lawyers through my wickets, thickets.
And ORDER, ORDER in the court.
But could they see me in the bath
Where I stand, mirrored, wet on scales!
Justice weighs itself, a fat fish
Of sixty: *Two hundred and four.*
This can't be me. Did she look so

When my morning's criminal struck
Off her head? Fish are not human.
And criminals? And I? I am a lover . . .
Of cards, croquet, the clock, and order,
Order in the court. I yearn to be
What I am, in robes . . . my bathrobe.
I take comfort in numerals.

The clock ticks like a heart. My heart
Ticks like a clock. Ice in my glass
Of bourbon clicks like dice. I shake
My fortune, my head. Grandfather chimes.
It's ten. I lock doors, windows,
Shut opinions in a briefcase,
Wind up Grandfather for tomorrow's
Judgment day. All is in order.
My wife completes her crossword puzzle.
The clock ticks. Dark. And all is well.

Swimming in bed I hear a noise.
Did I leave the faucet running?
Under the clock I hear a humming,
A stream flowing, line going out.
A feathered lure sinks through the ceiling.
Someone is trolling. I am dreaming.
I hear the clock and know it's raining.
Stars swim through wickets on our lawn.

Above the Supreme Court meets,
The Chief Justice, who wears no shoes,
Is setting the sun in his eye.
He strikes a ball through the wicket,
Winds his nose with a cloth. A cold
Today? What struck is now stricken.
And listen! The clock, the judge, says,
"Twelve."
        "Twelve what?" I ask. "Twelve fish
In season?"

"Just twelve!" Chimes the Judge
In his bathrobe and whacks the bench.
So it is. I roll in a ball.
The gavel strikes. My sentence dealt . . .
A million years and lives discarded.
It rains outside the house, the jail,
And order, order in the court.

CHARLEEN WHISNANT

To People Other Places, Gentlemen:

I wonder if you please would take the time
To write to me. I need to know
If people far away are just the same.

Here in the South the other day
A friend of mine, a doctor here
Dropped in to talk.
It was not long before he asked
"Do you believe in God?"
And I said sure because sometimes I do
And then I asked him why.
He might have come confused from seeing death
But he said no, a routine day
And thought about his question to himself.

Most people here say things like that
And ask each other what it means to die.
I thought that everybody did
Until a week ago when people came
Who lived in other countries all their lives.
They seemed surprised at us and said
They never had heard talk like that
And laughed.

I have been thinking ever since
About the place I live, about the South
And how I might not ever hear
What people other places know.

In Mexico, is anybody sure what life is for?
And in New York, where you have got to worry more
And get to talk, is there an answer?
If you know,
I wish that you would write and tell me so.

JAMES WHITEHEAD

Delta Farmer in a Wet Summer

Last summer was hot and dry, a better time—
Two cuttings at the dock and two knocked up
In the fields, and a crop to fill the wagons full.
There were prime steaks and politics at night—
Gin to nine and bourbon after that.
By God, we raised some handsome bales and hell,
Then went to New Orleans as usual.

But now it rains too long, too little sun
To stop the rot. Rain beats down on the roof
At night and gives sad dreams—black bolls—
And the Thunderbird will have to go. You can smell
It on the evenings, like the smell of a filthy
Bed, or wasted borrowed money, the stink
Of a bloated dog when finally the water's down.

. . . in California they say it's dry.
They irrigate consistently, don't count
The weather in when going to the bank,
And that's damned smart, except they've got no woods
Or sloughs to crowd the fields, and dogs get killed
But rarely drown—and I think our bitch, stretched hide
And stench, contains the element of chance a Christian needs.

One for the Road

Night full and the click of the lighter after love
   is almost kind and careless, too, like the laugh
   I leave with the sullen bills. And that's the way
   it is, if not the way it ought to be,
   down this Memphis road . . .

I ought not pay, I know,
   but your way of going is easier than most—
   and even now, after I pull first drag,
   you're not half bad, and next to the rig you're the best
   of love I've got. You're a little soft in the pooch—
   but, hell, I'm not a Natchez cock myself . . .

And it's not your legs or hair, God knows, not those,
   not easy things to get your mind around—
   it's your way of washing after all's got done,
   and something like fun among the common sounds—
   nails split, teeth gapped, who gives a damn . . .

And then the soft of loss with the coming sun,
   when you sleep me off like a dream almost of sin.

For a Neighbor Child

I yelled at you for climbing too high in our tree
   and descents like death confuse the memory
   and your falling face won't go and something more—
   the awful order of the past must be
   the necessary lie . . .

Up there at twelve you turned to kiss my son
    and now all's dark and you are younger than he.
    You had such courage, climbed the tree and fell—
    fell through limbs down thirty silent feet
    and all the age you'd learned . . .

And then you slept before you died
    and I have had to say you dreamed he'd fallen too . . .
    I could not miss your breaking skull
    and the few leaves your lover saw follow
    and you are constant in that fall . . .

A film in time continues to snap you up and down,
    a terrible reel that holds me still,
        for I praised when he wept against us great tears.

MILLER WILLIAMS

The Associate Professor
Delivers an Exhortation
to His Failing Students

Now when the frogs
that gave their lives for nothing
are washed from the brains and pans
we laid them in
I leave to you
who most excusably misunderstand
the margins of my talks
which because I am wise
and am a coward
were not appended to the syllabus

but I will fail to tell you
what I tell you
even before you fail to understand
so we might
in a manner of speaking
go down together.

I should have told you something of importance
to give at least a meaning
to the letter:

how, after hope, it sometimes happens

a girl, anonymous as beer,
telling forgotten things in a cheap bar

how she could have taught here as well as I.
Better.

The day I talked about the conduction of currents
I meant to say
be careful about getting hung up in the brain's things
that send you screaming like madmen through the town
or make you
like the man in front of the Jungle
that preaches on Saturday afternoons
a clown.

The day I lectured on adrenalin
I meant to tell you
as you were coming down
slowly out of the hills of certainty

empty your mind of the hopes that held you there.
Make a catechism of all your fears

and say it over:

this is the most of you . . . who knows . . . the best
where god was born
and heaven and confession
and half of love

From the fear of falling
and being flushed away
to the gulp of the suckhole and that rusting gut
from which no Jonah comes

that there is no Jesus and no hell

that god
square root of something equal to all
will not feel the imbalance when you fall

that rotting you will lie unbelievably alone
to be sucked up by some insignificant oak
as a child draws milk through straws
to be his bone.

These are the gravity that holds us together
toward our common sun

every hope getting out of hand
slings us hopelessly outward one by one
till all that kept us common is undone.

The day you took the test
I would have told you this:
that you had no time to listen for questions
hunting out the answers in your files
is surely the kind of irony
poems are made of

that all the answers at best are less than half

and you would have remembered
Lazarus
who hung around with god or the devil for days
and nobody asked him

anything

But if they do
If one Sunday morning they should ask you
the only thing that matters after all
tell them the only thing you know is true

tell them failing is an act of love
because
like sin
it is the commonality within

how failing together we shall finally pass
how to pomp and circumstance all of a class
noble of eye, blind mares between our knees,
lances ready, we ride to Hercules.

The day I said this had I meant to hope
some impossible punk on a cold slope
stupidly alone
would build himself a fire
to make of me an idiot

and a liar

CHARLES WRIGHT

The Bystanders

Always they sit
At the center of things,
Circles of conversation,
Camps of opinion,
Themselves so long
Housed in the outskirts
Of their own emotions they
Occupy there
Merely such neutral ground
As keeps their peace
Or honor. They leave
No fingermarks
On what their hands touch.
Their story is how they
Sidestep involvement, how
They stay of two minds
And how, finding
Themselves at last
Out in the open,
Maneuverings unsuccessful,
They answer only
What they don't feel,
What they don't know,
What they are not.

Reflections on
the Second Day of Spring

Held by the snow, which is cracked and wearing thin,
Is the head of a plastic horse, aquamarine.
There are no hooves, no tail: the body is missing.
A broken leather thong, once reins and the bit,
Lies on a sidewalk, half a yard away.
I try to imagine a child, but it, too, is missing:
In all of the afternoon there is no one else:
Only the horse whose body, somewhere, is running and
       running.

Contributors

ALVIN AUBERT is an associate professor of English at Southern University in Baton Rouge. He was born March 12, 1930, in Lutcher, Louisiana.

VAN K. BROCK was born in Barwick, Georgia, in 1932. Formerly in charge of the Undergraduate Poetry Workshop at the University of Iowa, he now teaches at Oglethorpe College in Atlanta.

ROBERT CANZONERI teaches at Ohio State University. A native of San Marcos, Texas, he has spent most of his life in Mississippi. He writes fiction, poetry, and drama, and is the author of *"I Do So Politely."*

RUTH DAWSON has received three *Atlantic Monthly* awards for her poems and an award from CBS for a television play. A native of Boyce, Louisiana, she is at present attending the University of Houston.

JAMES DICKEY, winner of the 1966 National Book Award for Poetry, was born in Atlanta in 1923. Mr. Dickey is now Consultant in Poetry for the Library of Congress. Among his volumes of poems are *Drowning With Others, Helmets,* and *Buckdancer's Choice.*

R. H. W. DILLARD teaches at Hollins College in Virginia and is an assistant editor of the *Transatlantic Review.* His first book, *The Day I Stopped Dreaming About Barbara Steele and Other Poems,* was published in 1966.

JEPTHA EVANS was born April 12, 1941, in Booneville, Arkansas. He was a student in the University of Iowa Writers' Workshop and now teaches English at California State College at Long Beach.

JEAN FARLEY lives near Roanoke, Virginia. Her poetry has been published in *Poetry*, the *New Yorker*, the *Hopkins Review*, the *Kenyon Review*, the *Southern Review*, and other magazines.

EDSEL FORD, a native of Alabama, is a freelance journalist living in Fort Smith, Arkansas. His books of poetry include *This Was My War*, *The Manchild from Sunday Creek*, *A Thicket of Sky*, and *Love Is the House It Lives In*.

JOHN FREEMAN was born December 20, 1942, in Jackson, Mississippi. Recipient of a Henry R. Bellamann Foundation Award, he is at present a graduate student at Mississippi College.

GEORGE GARRETT is the author of three novels, three collections of short stories, and three volumes of poems. Mr. Garrett teaches English at the University of Virginia and is poetry editor of the *Transatlantic Review*.

JANE GENTRY is an instructor in the English Department at Georgetown College, Georgetown, Kentucky. She was born in Lexington, Kentucky, in 1941 and studied at Hollins College and Brandeis University.

EDWIN GODSEY was born in 1930 in Bristol, Tennessee. He was teaching at the University of North Carolina at Charlotte when he contributed the work included here. Before the book went to press, Mr. Godsey drowned in a futile attempt to rescue his young son, who had fallen through the ice in a pond on the family's farm.

JEAN JEFFRIES was born in Spanish Fort, Mississippi, on May 25, 1937. She now lives in New York State, where her husband is a professor at Rensselaer Polytechnic Institute.

DONALD JUSTICE is the author of three volumes of poems, *Night Light*, *A Local Storm*, and *The Summer Anniversaries*, which was the Lamont Poetry Selection for 1959. Born in Miami in 1925, Mr. Justice teaches at Syracuse University.

RUTH LANEY was born in Baton Rouge on September 24, 1944. A recent graduate of Louisiana State University, she is currently doing graduate work at LSU in New Orleans.

ALFRED M. LEE was born in Louisville, Kentucky, which he still thinks of as home, though he has lived most recently in Paris. His work has appeared in such magazines as *Poetry*, the *Kenyon Review*, and the *Yale Review*.

DUANE LOCKE was born in Vienna, Georgia, in 1921. He now teaches at the University of Tampa, where he is the editor of *Poetry Review*.

VASSAR MILLER is the author of *Adam's Footprint, Wage War on Silence*, and *My Bones Being Wiser*, and is included in Louis Untermeyer's anthology of modern American poetry. A native of Houston, she is presently directing a writing workshop at St. John's School there.

MARION MONTGOMERY, a native of Georgia, has in recent years been associated with the University of Georgia Press, the *Georgia Review*, and the *Western Review*. He is the author of two novels and two books of poems.

HARRY MORRIS lives in Tallahassee, where he is professor of English at Florida State University. A volume of his poems, *The Sorrowful City*, was published in 1965.

TED-LARRY PEBWORTH, born April 19, 1938, in Shreveport, Louisiana, now teaches at the University of Illinois, Chicago. His work has appeared in *Targets, Motive*, and other magazines.

RONALD PERRY, a native of Miami, lives in Nassau, where he is an advertising and public relations executive. He is the author of *The Fire Nursery, The Rock Harbor, The Pipe Smokers*, and *Voyages From Troy*.

PATRICIA RACHAL was born in Baton Rouge and now lives in New Orleans. This is the first publication of her poetry.

PAUL RAMSEY was born November 26, 1924, in Atlanta. At present he is poet-in-residence at the University of Chattanooga. His most recent collection of poems was *In an Ordinary Place*.

LARRY RUBIN lives in Atlanta, where he is an associate professor of English at Emory. His first book of poems, *The World's Old Way*, received the Sidney Lanier Award and the Literary Achievement Award for Poetry.

JOSEPH EDGAR SIMMONS teaches at the University of Texas at El Paso. A native of Natchez, Mississippi, he is the author of *Pocahontas and Other Poems*.

MARCUS SMITH was born in Houston, Texas, in 1936. His poetry has been published in a number of magazines, and he has also received awards for drama. He is presently teaching at the American University in Beirut, Lebanon.

DABNEY STUART lives in Lexington, Virginia, and teaches at Washington and Lee University. A native of Richmond, he is the author of *The Diving Bell,* a collection of poems published in 1966.

HENRY TAYLOR is a native Virginian now teaching at Roanoke College. His first book of poems, *The Horse Show at Midnight,* was published in 1966. He is at work on a novel.

WILLIAM E. TAYLOR lives in DeLand, Florida, where he is a professor of English at Stetson University. He is the author of two volumes of poems, *Man in the Wind* and *Down Here with Aphrodite.*

ROBERT WATSON teaches at the University of North Carolina at Greensboro. He is the author of two books of poems, *A Paper Horse* and *Advantages of Dark,* and a novel, *Three Sides of the Mirror.*

CHARLEEN WHISNANT was born in Greensboro, North Carolina, and now lives in Charlotte. She is the editor of the *Red Clay Reader.* Her poems have appeared in the *Prairie Schooner* and other magazines.

JAMES WHITEHEAD teaches at the University of Arkansas. A native of St. Louis, he has spent much of his life in Mississippi. His first book of poems, *Domains,* was published in 1966.

MILLER WILLIAMS, co-editor of this volume and its companion volume of fiction, was born in Hoxie, Arkansas, in 1930. He is on the English faculty at Loyola University in New Orleans. Mr. Williams is the author of *A Circle of Stone.*

CHARLES WRIGHT was born August 25, 1935, in Pickwick Dam, Tennessee. His poems have appeared in the *New Yorker,* the *Nation,* the *North American Review,* and other magazines. At present he lives in Balboa Island, California.